© 2006 by
YouthLight, Inc.
Chapin, SC 29036

Project Editing by Susan Bowman

ISBN
1-889636-94-0

Library of Congress Number
2006901109

10 9 8 7 6 5 4 3 2 1
Printed in the United States

ABOUT THE AUTHOR AND ILLUSTRATOR

JON FILITTI, MA LMHC, CREATOR AND AUTHOR

Jon Filitti is a mental health counselor and has been working with youth and families for 10 years. He currently works in Dubuque, Iowa. Presently, his positions include Outpatient Therapist, Resource Mapping Coordinator for Severely Emotionally Disturbed Children, and Family Support Program Coordinator for eighteen Dubuque Community schools. Jon has also designed, developed, and maintained www.youthpsych.com, an online community website offering support and information for parents and professionals. Jon has also developed the website www.ootwcomic.com, to enhance the "Out of This World" series.

ERIC ERBES, ILLUSTRATOR

Born and raised in the San Francisco bay area Eric studied illustration at Cogswell College in Sunnyvale, California. Upon graduating in 2001 Eric dabbled in a variety of jobs including animator, card designer and video game tester before deciding to pursue a full-time career in comics. Before 'Out of this World' he had experience working in almost all aspects of the comics field including lettering for Viz Comics, coloring for Ablaze Media, and illustrating for About Comics. Eric currently works as a freelance artist in sunny Santa Cruz, California.

Leader Guide

This Leader Guide has been created to guide you, page by page, in achieving OOTW's full potential in working with youth. Each lesson contains suggested discussion areas and questions.

Lesson 1: Pages 2-6

Objective: Identifying Personal Strengths.

1. Questions for this Lesson are contained within the Activity.

Lesson 2: Pages 7-10

Objective: Goal Setting and Getting Started.

1. Have you ever tried to set goals for yourself, either at home or at school? If you have, what was the experience like? Was setting goals helpful?
2. If setting goals did not work, is there a reason why you think they failed to help?
3. Sometimes adults may "force" goals on you. Why do you think they do this? Is it helpful? Do you think they are trying to help you by making you motivated?

Lesson 3: Pages 11-16

Objective: Making your Motivation Obvious to Others.

1. Some of these words are rather large and may be difficult to understand. Which words are difficult to understand?
2. What do these words mean to you? How can we define these words? Also, how do they relate back to the word "Motivation"?
3. Now that these words are understood, how have you used them in your life?

Lesson 4: Pages 17-20

Objective: Determination and Persistence.

1. Sometimes all the Determination in the world won't solve some of the more difficult problems that life throws you. When that happens you need what is called Persistence. What does persistence mean to you?
2. Were you frustrated when you worked hard on the (Determination) activity, only to find that you needed another answer? How does this happen in your life?
3. Persistence is sometimes hard to going after. Hurdles like frustration, tiredness, lack of time, and others, get in the way of being persistently motivated. What are some ways that you can overcome these "hurdles"?

Lesson 5: Pages 21-27

Objective: Being Resourceful, Knowing Who to go to.

1. We see here that all the characters in the story work together to beat the ice creatures. If you had to draw an activity like this, but only included the people in your life, who would be on this list? Have the child write them in the spaces provided.
2. How does working with a partner, team, or adult help to increase your own motivation?
3. Besides other people, what else can you do to become more motivated? Make a list of these ideas to keep with you.

Lesson 6: Pages 28-30

Objective: Learning from Success, Using it in future situations, and Learning from Rewards.

1. What is reinforcement or reward? Did you feel a sense of accomplishment after completing this activity and this book? Even though it was difficult at times you made it through. You should be proud of yourself.
2. Can reinforcement be something other than money or items that someone gives you? If so, list some ideas.
3. Max feels very proud of himself at the end of this issue. Have you ever felt proud of yourself after you persisted were successful? If so, does being proud of yourself count for being reinforced? And if so, does it increase the chances that you will be more easily motivated and determined in the future since you have already seen you can be successful at it?

4

Fine.

What would you do?

For starters, I wouldn't just be sitting here.

You need to figure out what your strengths are so you can use them to fix this.

And how should I do that?

I have no clue. But I know you won't do it feeling sorry for yourself.

I know!

I need to find Marcania and see what needs to be done.

Sounds like a start.

Just stop moping and get motivated.

Go get him Max.

Go get Tiglos!

MY LIST OF STRENGTHS!

Hope is encouraging Max to become motivated and work through the problem that he has created. In order to do this, Max must find what his strengths are and put them to good use. We all have strengths, some that we may not even know about. But in order to be successful, in order to become motivated, we need to learn what our strengths are. Please use another sheet of paper if you need additional space.

1. Working with a parent, teacher, counselor, or group, begin writing down what your strengths are. Challenge yourself to come up with every one that you can think of.

_____

2. Compare your list with the ideas of others. What strengths were on both lists?

_____

3. What strengths did you forget? Two of Max's strengths are caring and determination.

_____

4. What strengths did others not list? Why do you think they do not see these strengths?

_____

5. What is one of your biggest motivators in life?

_____

6. Who are some people in your life that help you feel motivated?

_____

7. Discuss some ways that you have been motivated in the past. Discuss the success that you've had due to motivation.

_____

_____

8. What do you find rewarding, and how can you use these rewards to increase your motivation?

_____

_____

_____

Come on! Somebody figure it out!

Wait a second...

ERROR: UNKNOWN COORDINATES

THE MOTIVATION CREATOR!

We see that Max is determined to fix the mess he created. Notice he doesn't need anyone else telling him to be motivated about this problem. He's simply motivated to work on the problem.

So why does motivation only happen sometimes? Wouldn't it be nice if we could be motivated all of the time? Is that even possible? Let's figure out how you can create your own personal motivation.

Most of us are not self-motivators all the time, which means we have to find ways to get excited about being successful. We do this by setting goals. Goals give us something to work toward, something to strive for. They are very helpful in assisting you in paying attention, which is crucial for motivation. This activity will assist you in learning how to set and meet goals.

DIRECTIONS:

(1) Problem: Write about what you want to change.

(2) Goal: Write what your behavior would look like when you change.

(3) Plan: Make a plan of how you will meet your goal.

(4) Who will help: Think of anyone that can help and ask them.

(5) Reward: Make sure that you choose something that's exciting!

Problem: _____

Goal: _____

Plan: _____

Who will help: _____

Reward: _____

EXAMPLE:

Problem: I have a difficult time completing my homework.

Goal: I will complete my homework right after school.

Plan: I will do my homework when I get home before playing.

Who will help: My parent will remind me when I get home.

Reward: If I'm able to meet this goal for one whole week I will be allowed to go outside for 1 hour longer.

10 *Remember, your motivation is to work for your reward!

Meanwhile...

LESSON 3: MAKING YOUR MOTIVATION OBVIOUS TO OTHERS.

Finally...

...some fighting room.

AHHHGH!

KLANK

Not gonna break huh?

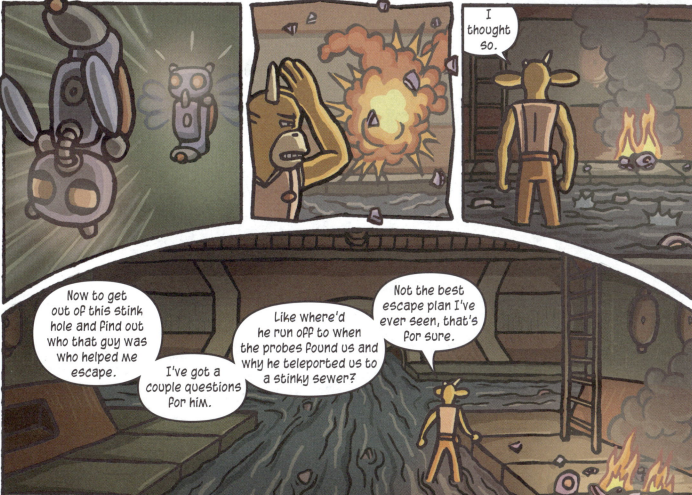

WORD FIND MOTIVATION!

Below you will see a word find activity. Your goal is to find the words that demonstrate motivation, which are listed at the bottom of the page. Being able to understand these words will assist you in telling and showing others that you are motivated.

```
S R N P A G H I F D E T E R M I N A T I O C
N E Y H N E W W T N S I H L E C B D P G P N
L E S R Q Z T I V I B N T M F Q E G C N R D
I H S C Y L E A Q C B D S S M A Q I J Q I D
N D E S I R E Q A Y S O L I G E A N N O D E
C H N H Z T N N A I E T L O E T I S F L E V
E T N I H Z Z E R H O P U C I T L P I H D O
N A S A R H Q E E J E A T R A T E I D D E T
T C H L E P A S S I O N M I O A H R E E H I
I C D A A K I P I N M Q A R A N E A N A E O
V P A M B I T I O N C E N D S N T T C U P N
E N T Y S N S M A N H C S A E S P I E T H S
A B R B A G S A A S A I Y S P L Y O C I T A
V F O C U S R S T L E E T E P I M N T E D T
M H Y G A T T I P E R S I S T A N C E P C I
A N O V A E T I P S T H E L E A P T M N T A
```

HIDDEN WORDS:

DESIRE	PRIDE
INSPIRATION	AMBITION
PERSISTANCE	DETERMINATION
INCENTIVE	DEVOTION
PASSION	FOCUS

14

Meanwhile...

Why can't I figure this out?

Soon...

16

This is it Max.

LESSON 4: DETERMINATION & PERSISTENCE

This is the point where I usually lose you.

Right here.

This problem is harder than the rest. It's okay to be challenged. It's okay to not get the answer right away.

I don't mind having to work a little bit, but this one is impossible!

That's because you give up too easily.

You have to stay motivated until you meet your goal.

I am motivated, it's just, there's no answer for this.

There will always be an answer for any situation Max, as long as you stick with it. Trust me.

I don't know Mr. Fischer.

Max, just because you haven't found the answer doesn't mean there isn't one.

Stay motivated and you'll find it.

17

THE WINNING FORMULA!

Max is trying to figure out the formula in order to find Tiglos, but he only has Raw Data. He's come up with a method of coding the Raw Data but he needs your help to find the answer.

Step 1: Add up the Raw Data numbers in each column and each row.

For Example: In Column I add the numbers 1, 3, 4, 7 and 2.
In Row VI add the numbers 1, 2, 1, 0 and 4.

RAW DATA:	I	II	III	IV	V	TOTAL
VI	1	2	1	0	4	▶
VII	3	6	0	4	7	▶
VIII	4	8	9	5	0	▶
IX	7	3	1	3	8	▶
X	2	4	5	1	5	▶
TOTAL	▼	▼	▼	▼	▼	

Step 2: Enter the answers into Row A below.

Step 3: Convert the *Row A* numbers to letters using the chart below as a guide. Enter these letters into *Row B* above. Example: 11=k.

	I	II	III	IV	V	VI	VII	VIII	IX	X
A										
B										

1	A	6	F	11	K	15	O	19	S	23	W
2	B	7	G	12	L	16	P	20	T	24	X
3	C	8	H	13	M	17	Q	21	U	25	Y
4	D	9	I	14	N	18	R	22	V	26	Z

Step 4: Use the letters in *Row B* to complete the activity on the next page.

HAVE SOME DIRECTION!

Are you still motivated? I hope so, because that was only the first part to finding Tiglos. Now write the answer from *Row B* (page 18) into the Coordinates box below. Then connect the dots on the map. If done correctly the coordinates will point right to Tiglos location. So stay motivated, be persistent, and find Tiglos!

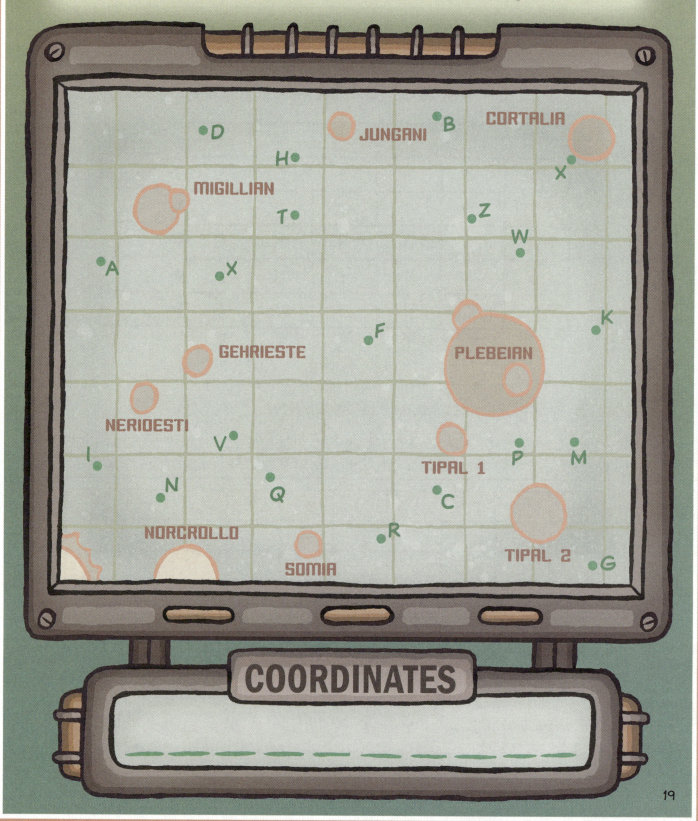

CORTALIA

JUNGANI

MIGILLIAN

GEHRIESTE

NERIDESTI

NORCROLLO

SOMIA

PLEBEIAN

TIPAL 1

TIPAL 2

COORDINATES

— — — — — — — —

20

Planet Cortalia...

LESSON 5:
BEING RESOURCEFUL,
KNOWING WHO CAN HELP.

Now to get out of here without being seen.

The coast looks clear.

AROOOOGA

Look up there!

22

26

LEAN ON ME!

Just like you and me, Tiglos could really use his friend's help. Help him find the right path to Max and Marcania.

...and then Tiglos came up behind it and...

I HAVE LEARNED A LOT ABOUT HUMANITY FROM MAX.

Are you kidding me Bogs?

I know, I know, he's human scum.

But you know, I have to give the little squirt some credit.

Max, I want to apologize for yelling at you before.

I was just—

You don't have to be sorry.

You were right, I messed up.

I should be the one saying sorry to Tiglos for missing his distress call in the first place.

Hey, why all the sad talk?

Let's celebrate. You did good Max.

You stepped up when we needed you most.

I'm here, we're safe.

29

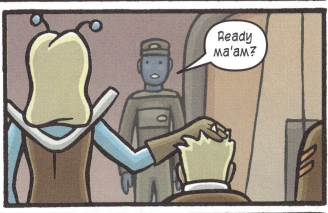

Hello again and welcome to the end of the first story arc of "Out of This World". Both Eric and I are excited to have completed the first four issues and finally give Max a happy ending. However, he still has a lot of work to do in order to get back home to Earth. There are many more adventures ahead for Max and his friends. Plus there are many more lessons for him to learn along the way.

We'd like to thank all of you for the positive response we've received about the comic books. We're happy to be able to use comics to educate and help kids and look forward to many more opportunities. If you've read OOTW issues #1-4, make sure that you visit our website at www.ootwcomic.com. The site offers many interesting pages, like Behind the Scenes, Sketch Art, Character Profiles and even Fan Art! We will also be keeping you updated for more comics that may be coming in the future.

Well, that's all for now. If you have any questions or just want to say hi, make sure to e-mail me at jon@ootwcomic.com.

Thanks for reading and learning with us!

Jon Filitti and Eric Erbes